W9-CHM-809

Paper Cars

Nine Cool Cars That You Can Make.
Just colour, cut, fold and paste!

CONTENTS

Copyright © 2010 by Sam Atwal

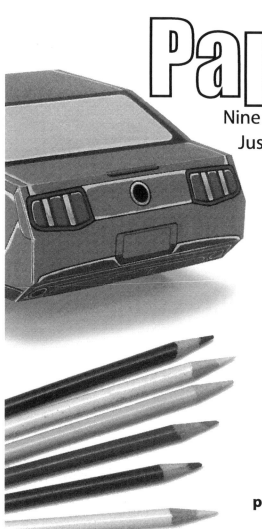

Paper Cars

Nine Cool Cars That You Can Make.
Just colour, cut, fold and paste!

CONTENTS

Smart Car
Mini Cooper 'S'
Ford Mustang
Lamborghini Gallardo
Hummer H2
BMW Z8
Ferrari Testarossa
Bentley Continental GT
Porsche 911 Turbo

TOOLS

scissors or X-acto knife
metal ruler
pencil crayons and markers
glue stick

DIRECTIONS

1. **PRINT** or **PHOTOCOPY** each page on to **CARD STOCK**

2. Use scissors and carefully **CUT OUT** the page that you are working on.

3. Use your x-acto knife and metal ruler to carefully **SCORE** all of your folds **BEFORE** you start colouring.

4. **COLOUR** in your car. **PRESS HARD** to get nice, rich colour. Leave some white areas for highlights. **DO NOT COLOUR** over the glue areas and the small square box where the MIRRORS will go.

5. Carefully **CUT OUT** your car using the x-acto knife or scissors.

6. **FOLD** all of your tabs and see how things line up.

7. Use a glue stick to **GLUE** your car together.

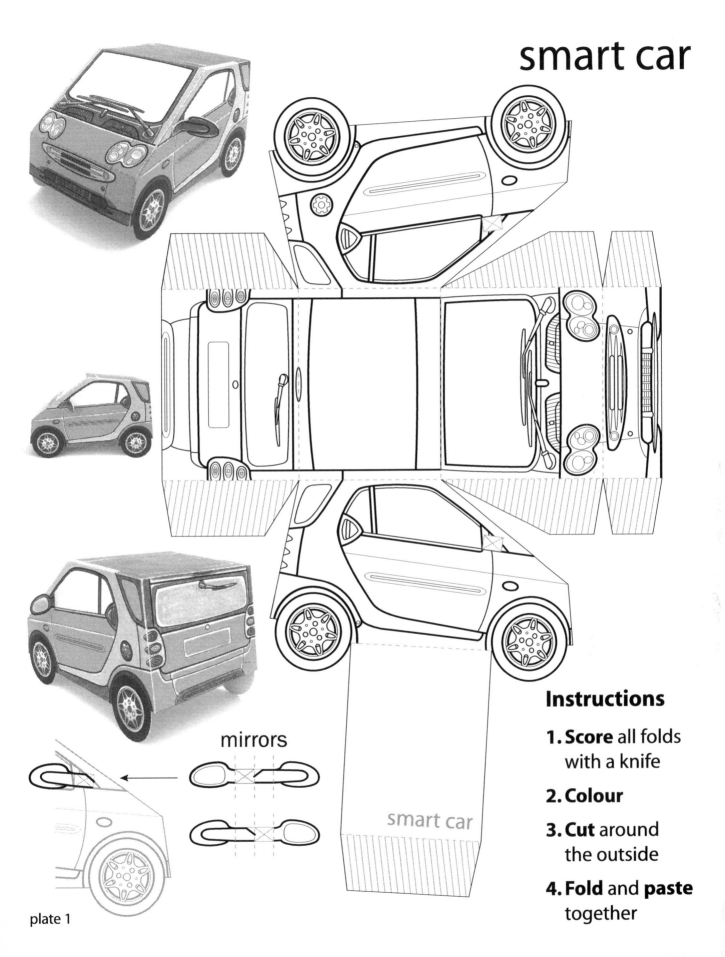

smart car

mirrors

Instructions

1. **Score** all folds with a knife

2. **Colour**

3. **Cut** around the outside

4. **Fold** and **paste** together

smart car

plate 1

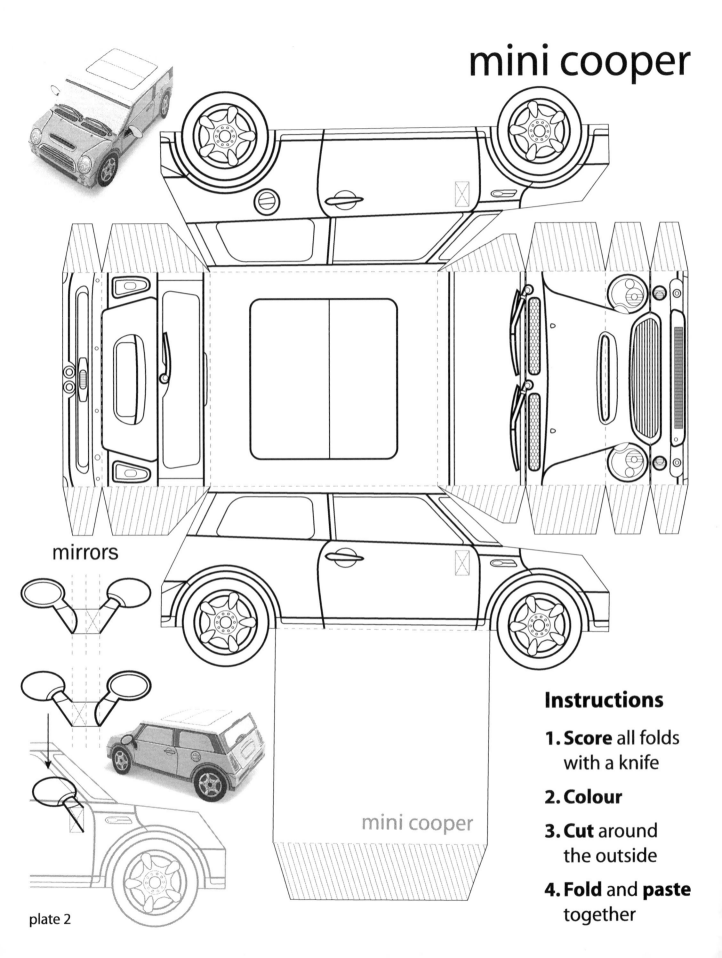

mini cooper

mirrors

Instructions

1. **Score** all folds with a knife

2. **Colour**

3. **Cut** around the outside

4. **Fold** and **paste** together

mini cooper

plate 2

ford mustang

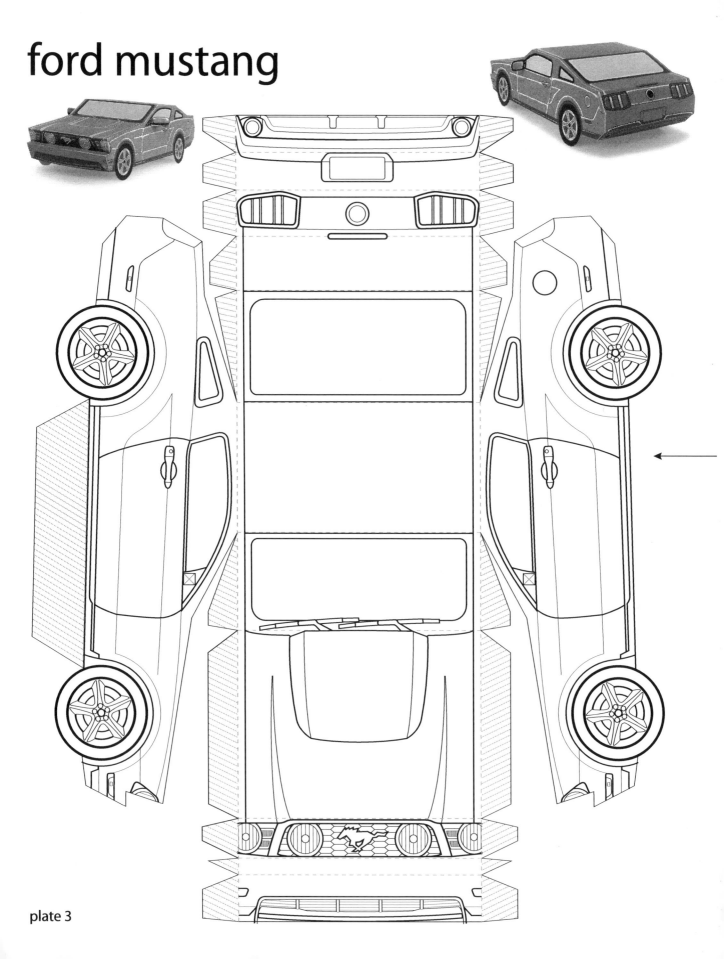

plate 3

ford mustang

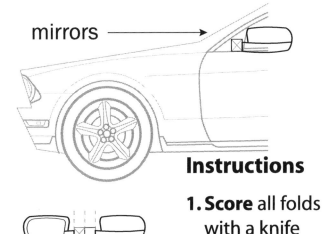

mirrors

Instructions

1. **Score** all folds with a knife
2. **Colour**
3. **Cut** around the outside
4. **Fold** and **paste** together

ford mustang

paste this piece underneath

lamborghini gallardo

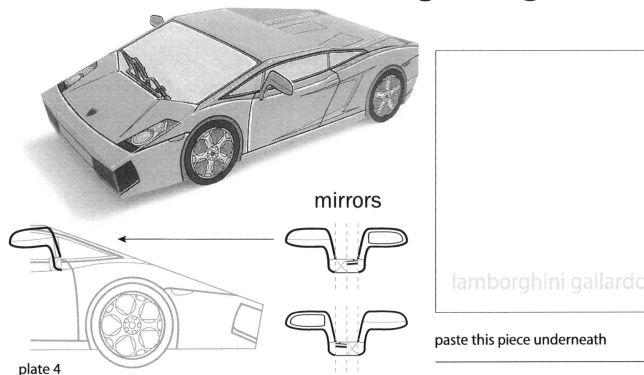

mirrors

lamborghini gallardo

paste this piece underneath

plate 4

lamborghini gallardo

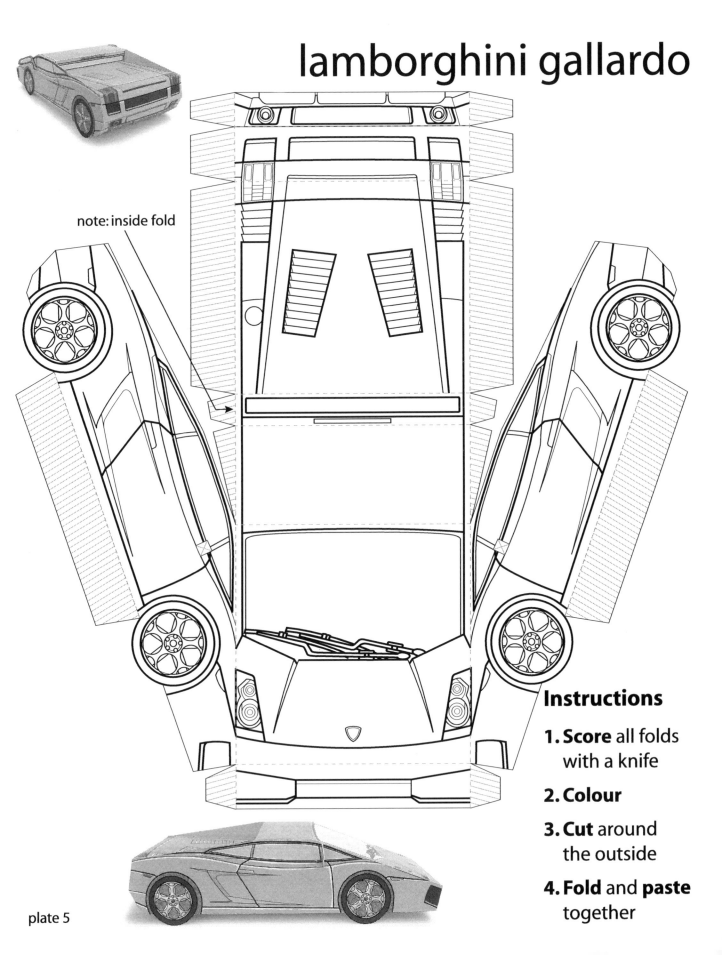

note: inside fold

Instructions

1. **Score** all folds with a knife

2. **Colour**

3. **Cut** around the outside

4. **Fold** and **paste** together

plate 5

hummer h2

mirrors

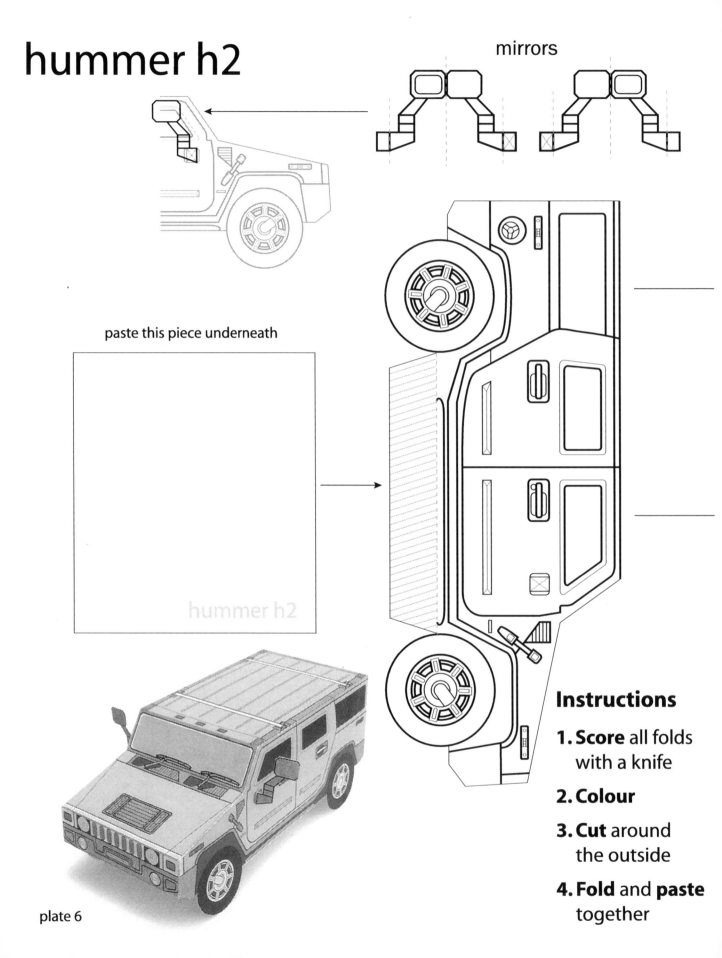

paste this piece underneath

hummer h2

Instructions

1. **Score** all folds with a knife

2. **Colour**

3. **Cut** around the outside

4. **Fold** and **paste** together

plate 6

hummer h2

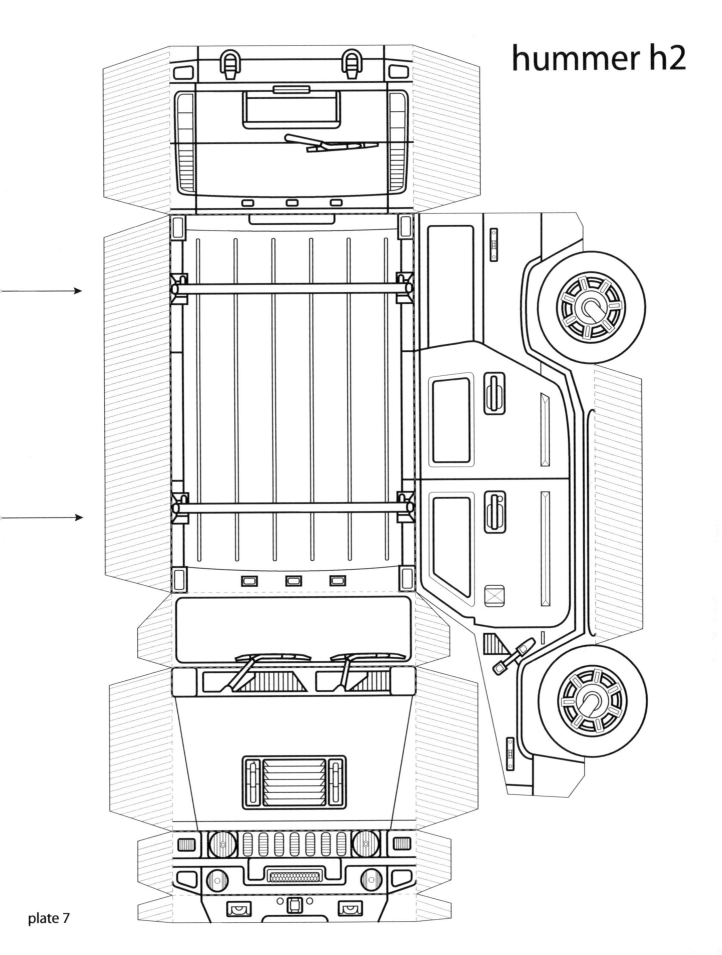

plate 7

bmw z8

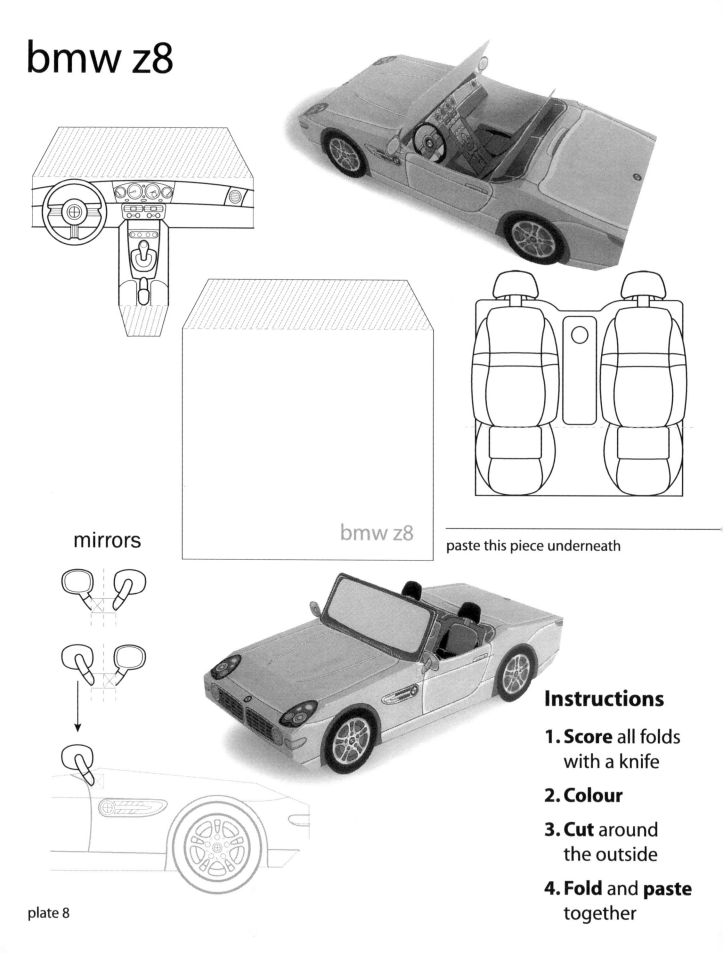

mirrors

bmw z8

paste this piece underneath

Instructions

1. **Score** all folds with a knife

2. **Colour**

3. **Cut** around the outside

4. **Fold** and **paste** together

plate 8

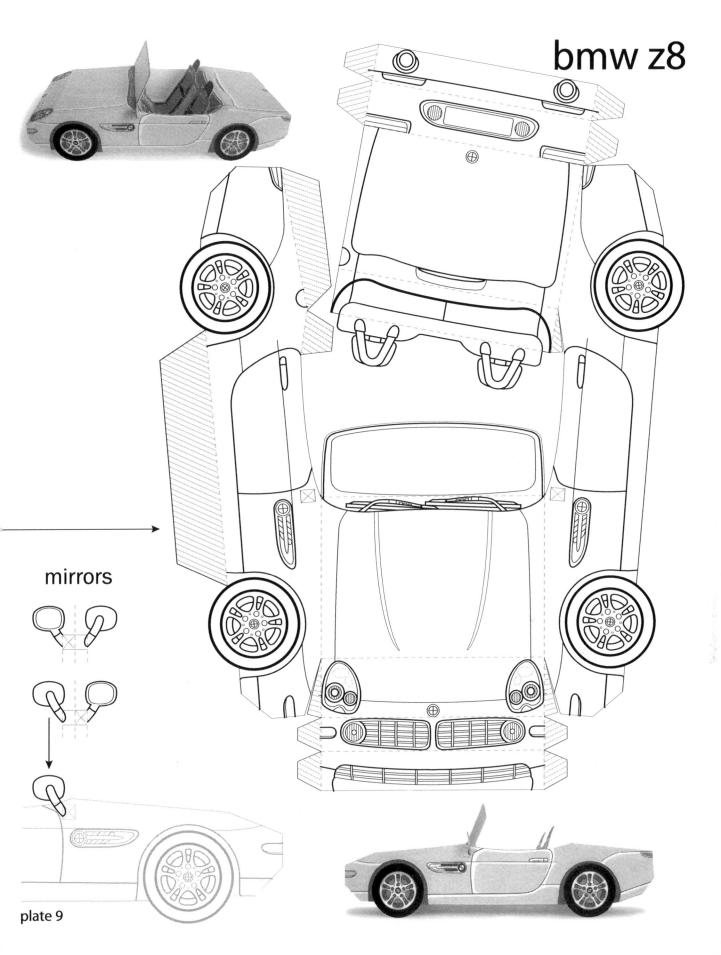

bmw z8

mirrors

plate 9

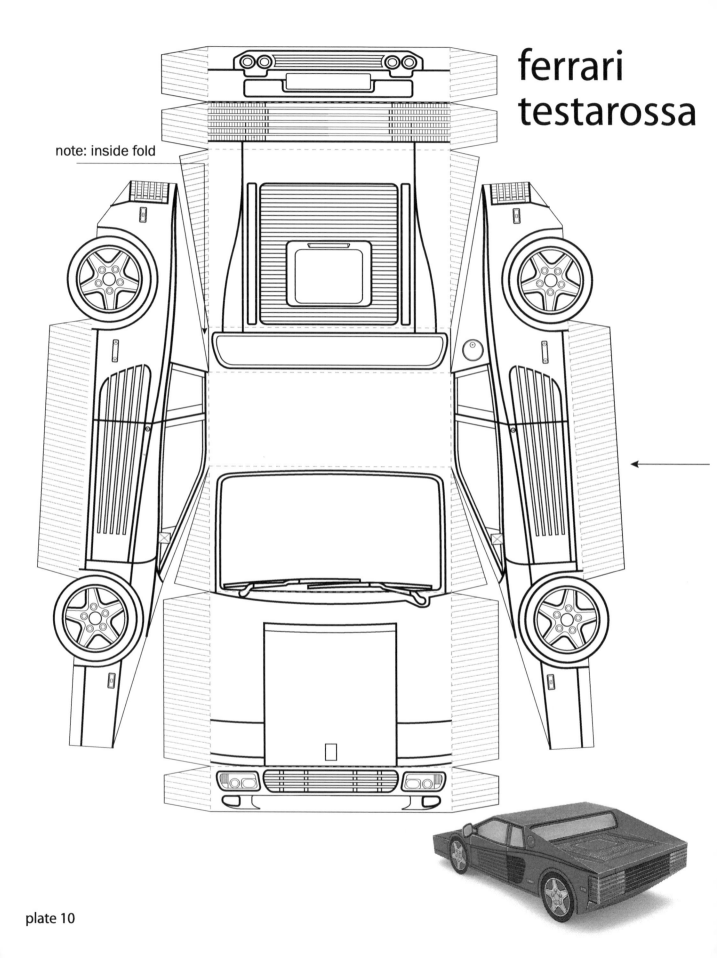

ferrari
testarossa

note: inside fold

plate 10

ferrari testarossa

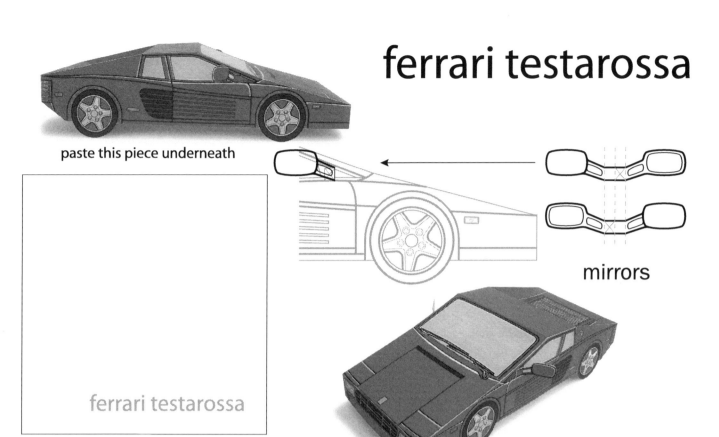

paste this piece underneath

ferrari testarossa

mirrors

bentley continental gt

mirrors

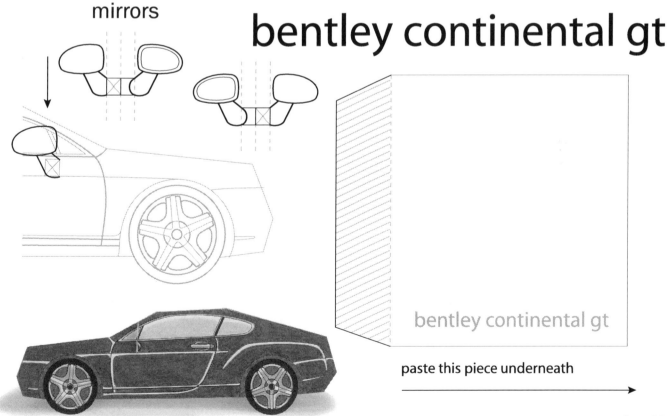

bentley continental gt

paste this piece underneath

plate 11

bentley continental gt

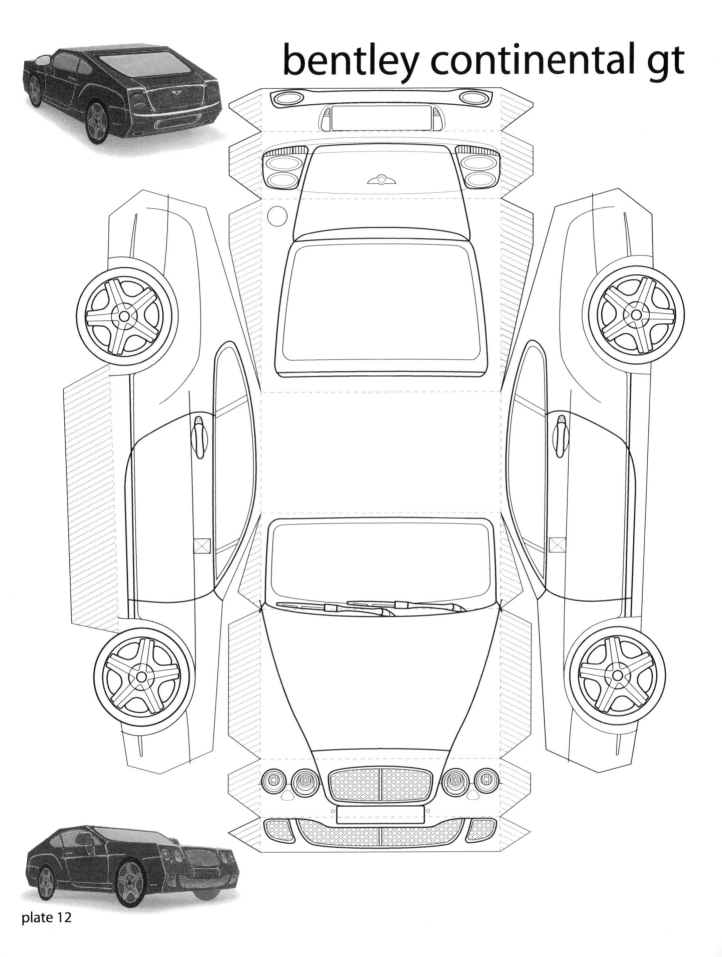

plate 12

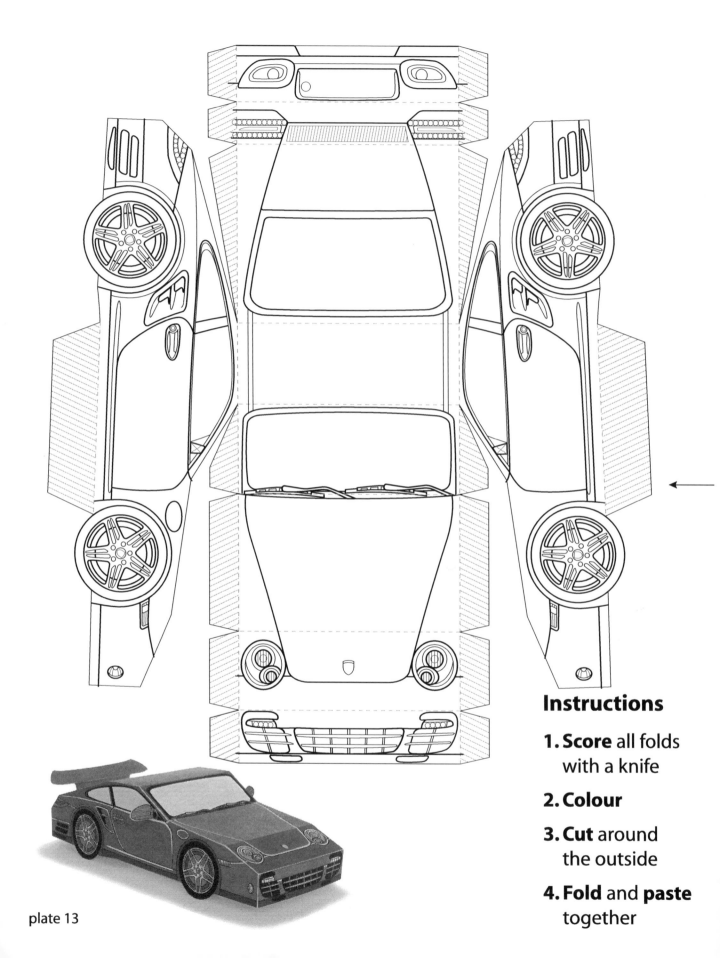

Instructions

1. **Score** all folds with a knife

2. **Colour**

3. **Cut** around the outside

4. **Fold** and **paste** together

plate 13

porsche 911 turbo

porsche 911 turbo

paste this piece underneath

mirrors

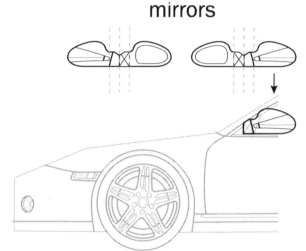

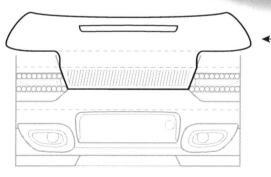

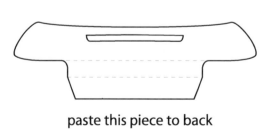

paste this piece to back

plate 14

Coming Soon
Paper SportsCars!

Copyright © 2010 by Sam Atwal

35371362R10020

Made in the USA
Lexington, KY
08 September 2014